HISTORY'S
VILLAINS

IDI
AMIN

John Allen

BLACKBIRCH®
PRESS

THOMSON

GALE

San Diego • Detroit • New York • San Francisco • Cleveland • New Haven, Conn. • Waterville, Maine • London • Munich

LIBRARY OF CONGRESS CATALOGING-IN-PUBLICATION DATA

Allen, John, 1957-
  Idi Amin / by John Allen.
    p. cm. — (History's villains)
Includes index.
Summary: Describes the events leading to Idi Amin's rise to power, his brutal reign as Uganda's president, how he was ousted, and what happened in Uganda afterwards.
  ISBN 1-56711-759-7 (hardback : alk. paper)
  1. Amin, Idi, 1925—Juvenile literature. 2. Presidents—Uganda—Biography—Juvenile literature. 3. Uganda—History—1971-1979—Juvenile literature. [1. Amin, Idi, 1925- 2. Presidents—Uganda. 3. Uganda—History—1971-1979.] I. Title. II. Series.

  DT433.28.A45A45 2004
  967.6104'2'092--dc22

                                                    2003014716

Printed in the United States
10 9 8 7 6 5 4 3 2 1

CONTENTS

INTRODUCTION: "A BRUTAL REGIME"

On a sunny morning in Kampala, Uganda, in 1974, a man named Michael Ondoga drove his daughter, Peace, to school. In front of the school building, a black car pulled up alongside Ondoga's automobile. Ondoga recognized the car as belonging to the State Research Bureau, the notorious agency of Uganda's president, General Idi Amin Dada. Several men in sunglasses spilled out and surrounded Ondoga's car. They shouted at him to get out. When he did, they began to beat him up. Many people looked on—teachers, parents, children, and Ondoga's own daughter. All were paralyzed with fear. For the adults, this was a familiar scene in their city. Ondoga was wrestled into the black car, and it raced away. One of the agents stayed behind to take Ondoga's car for himself.

Ondoga's crime had been to draw the disfavor of Amin, the military dictator of Uganda. Ondoga had been named Amin's minister of foreign affairs immediately after the coup in 1971 that brought Amin to power. Since then, for no discernible reason, Amin had turned against the man. Uneasy from hearing stories about shadowy assassinations, Ondoga had hired bodyguards to protect him. This step only increased Amin's anger. When, at an official ceremony, Amin announced that he was replacing Ondoga, other ministers feared for Ondoga's life.

After the incident outside the school, Ondoga was not seen for several days. Finally his body turned up in the morgue of the Jinja Hospital. Ondoga had been shot several times, stabbed, his skull was crushed in, and his ribs were broken. He had also been dumped in water—perhaps in Lake Victoria or the Nile River, where many of Amin's victims ended up. The general placed guards at the morgue to keep Ondoga's relatives from claiming the body. Burial was handled by Amin's soldiers.

What happened to Michael Ondoga was repeated hundreds and even thousands of times in the eight years of Idi Amin's brutal regime. Amin, who gained power through a network of military and tribal allies, ruled with a haphazard system of terror and revenge against his enemies. He plunged Uganda into a nightmare from which it is still struggling to recover.

Idi Amin seized power in Uganda in 1971, killed more than three hundred thousand people, and left the country in economic ruin.

CHAPTER 1

INDEPENDENCE FOR UGANDA

The East African country of Uganda is a beautiful land rich in resources. British prime minister Winston Churchill once called it "the pearl of Africa." Yet the people of Uganda have undergone terrible hardships under brutal rulers. The most notorious of these was General Idi Amin Dada, who took power in a military coup in 1971. His murderous regime is estimated to have killed three hundred thousand people, and it plunged Uganda into a cycle of violence and misery that continues today.

Opposite: Idi Amin seized power in a military coup in 1971, and brutally ruled Uganda for eight years.

The Four Kingdoms

For hundreds of years, the tribes that lived in the East African land that became Uganda were grouped into eight separate kingdoms. A native Ugandan owed his or her first loyalty to the kingdom. The four largest kingdoms were the lands of Buganda, Bunyoro, Ankole, and Toro. The most powerful of these was the kingdom of Buganda. Its people were Baganda, the largest tribe in all of Uganda. The Baganda's hereditary king, called a *kabaka*, ruled the kingdom of Buganda through a large network of chieftains and councils.

The last great king of Buganda was Mutesa I, who began his rule in the mid-1800s. He was widely respected for his fairness and wisdom as king; members

While Mutesa I ruled the kingdom of Buganda, he encouraged his people to trade and live peacefully with European newcomers. This eighteenth-century woodcut depicts a Ugandan king reviewing his troops.

of other tribes often brought their disputes to him. As contacts with European explorers and missionaries increased, Mutesa I recognized that his people could no longer live in isolation. He encouraged trade with outsiders and worked peacefully with the European newcomers. Many of his people converted to Christianity. Mutesa's vision for the future included a rich exchange of goods, culture, and ideas with Europeans.

British Exploitation

Europe's rulers, however, saw Africa as a source of wealth to be exploited. In the late 1800s, European diplomats who had never set foot in Africa divided the eastern part into "spheres of influence" to be controlled by European nations. No thought was given to tribal boundaries when Uganda became a protectorate of Great Britain— an area under British control and protection. Tribes with little in common except loyalty to their own kingdoms were grouped together in the new configurations. Despite British rule, the tribal leadership in the four kingdoms, particularly Buganda, continued to exert a powerful influence over their people.

The British introduced cottonseed to Uganda and began to create a system for exporting cotton to Europe. They set up tenant farms with the help of Buganda's chieftains, and then they forced workers to build a railway to haul cotton crops to the eastern coast of Africa. Uganda's abundant rain and fertile soil helped the plan succeed. Goods from Great Britain, such as furniture, clothes, and bicycles, became widely available, and schools improved rapidly.

Nevertheless, resentment toward the British grew among native Ugandans. Peasant farmers received less than half of the profits from their crops. People distrusted the protectorate government that cared more about British wealth than about the people's welfare. They complained that Asian and white immigrants were rewarded with better jobs and more business than natives. During World War II, when Britain's attentions were focused elsewhere, Ugandans began to clamor for independence.

The movement gained speed in 1952 when Great Britain appointed a new governor for Uganda. Sir Andrew Cohen made changes that would lead to self-government for the people. The number of Africans on the legislative council, Uganda's ruling body, was increased. Political parties sprang up, and independence seemed close at hand.

Buganda and King Freddie

Before a change of government could take place, the issue of what to do about the kingdoms had to be

When King Freddie (right), or Mutesa II, and British governor Sir Andrew Cohen (left) disagreed about how to unite Uganda's kingdoms, Cohen exiled the king to England.

settled. In particular, the kingdom of Buganda, with its large population of Baganda tribespeople, continued to have a great influence on Uganda's politics. In 1953 Mutesa II (known to the Baganda as King Freddie) disputed with Cohen over his plan for a unified state. King Freddie and many of his people feared they would lose their dominance and prosperity. Frustrated with King Freddie's stubbornness, Cohen ordered him exiled to England, a move that outraged the Baganda. Although the king was allowed to return in two years, the damage was lasting. The Buganda kingdom became even more belligerent about what it saw as its superior position in the country. From time to time, King Freddie threatened to create his own Bugandan state.

Milton Obote, a Langi tribesman and leader of the independence movement, saw the influence of Buganda in Ugandan politics as a potential obstacle to his own rise to power. Obote led the Uganda People's Congress (UPC), one of the country's two major political parties. The other major party was made up of Buganda loyalists with dreams of their own separate nation. Obote negotiated a plan for Buganda to remain part of the unified state of Uganda. King Freddie was allowed to be the ceremonial head of the new nation. On October 9, 1962, Uganda celebrated its full independence. After elections were held, the two major parties formed a coalition. Obote became prime minister of a free Uganda.

Conflict and a Revolt

It was not long before the optimism created by independence turned to conflict. Obote came from a small ethnic group in the north, the Langi. In a country where ethnic and tribal loyalties count for so much, he lacked ties to the larger, more powerful groups. To compensate, Obote filled his government with representatives from many groups, and each demanded special favors for his region or people. In addition, there were other kinds of tensions. Livestock farmers in the north complained that crop farmers in the south received much more government help. With native Africans in power, there was a backlash against Christianity, seen by some as a "white" religion. There was a corresponding increase in Muslim influence, although Muslims made up only about 10 percent of the population. Christians, who had thrived under British rule, now felt pushed aside.

In 1964, the unstable situation got worse. Some units of the Uganda army revolted against Obote's government, demanding higher pay and promotions. Obote turned to British troops to quell the uprising. Great Britain agreed to help, mainly because it was Uganda's main trading partner. While the new government was saved, Obote realized he could not keep power without strong

Milton Obote, the first prime minister of a free Uganda, called in British troops to put down the 1964 uprising of the Ugandan army.

support from the military. He granted all the army's demands in exchange for its loyalty.

With independence, many educated Ugandans had hoped that democracy would take root in their country. Now those hopes were rapidly fading. With the military solidly behind him, Obote no longer needed to compromise with his opponents. Instead of offering favors and making promises to bring groups together, he simply resorted to threats of force. Obote quickly became a dictator instead of a prime minister.

Amin's Early Life

One Ugandan officer in particular won Obote's notice for his loyal support. The officer's name was Idi Amin Dada. The details of Amin's early life are sketchy. The exact year of his birth is disputed, but it was probably 1925 or 1926. Amin was born in Koboko County in Uganda's northwest district, west of the Nile River. He was a member of the Kakwa, a tribe of about fifty thousand. The Kakwa are a small tribe in Uganda, but much larger numbers of Kakwa live in Congo and southern Sudan. The arid land in Amin's home region supports little economic activity but herding, and the people there are notoriously warlike. For years, the area had been a popular recruiting ground for soldiers.

UGANDA, A LAND OF NATURAL BEAUTY

The African nation of Uganda is roughly the size of the state of Oregon. Its many lakes and rivers include Lake Victoria, which forms part of its southern border. Almost a third of the country is covered by water. Its diverse landscape is due to its location where the East African savanna and the West African rain forest zones overlap. There are mountain chains on the eastern, western, and northern borders, lush hills with thick vegetation in the central area, and dry savanna in the northeast. Uganda is also home to some of the world's most dramatic waterfalls.

Although Uganda is crossed by the equator, its climate is relatively mild because of its elevation. Temperatures in the northern plain exceed eighty-six degrees Fahrenheit (thirty degrees Celcius), while on the central plateau, depending on the elevation, they range from sixty to eighty degrees Fahrenheit (sixteen to twenty-seven degrees Celcius). Rainfall is abundant but seasonal. Wet seasons occur in April and May and again in October and November. Most of the country is green all year round.

Uganda's natural diversity also extends to its plants and animals. The tropical rain forests of western Uganda feature a staggering array of exotic plants. Nature trails offer tourists the chance to explore these areas at their leisure. Uganda also has many national parks and game preserves, where visitors can see elephants, rhinos, giraffes, gorillas, leopards, cheetahs, and many other species. The country holds more than one thousand bird species, which is almost half of all species in Africa. The Queen Elizabeth National Park alone has more than five hundred different kinds of birds. In fact, the crested crane is the national emblem, and is depicted on the Ugandan flag.

The hippos in this river are just one of the variety of animals that live in Uganda's many national parks and game preserves.

Village tales declare that midwives worked for many hours to deliver Idi. He was reportedly a huge baby of twelve pounds. While he was still an infant, his mother took him and ran away from his father. The years that followed were difficult. Idi's mother, a member of the Lugbara, a Sudanese tribe, moved with Idi to her home district and worked on an estate where sugarcane was grown. Later, she became involved with Yafesi Yasin. Yasin was a clerk in the King's African Rifles (KAR), a unit of native Africans in the British colonial forces. Idi and his mother lived in the army barracks. When Yasin grew tired of her and tried to dismiss her, Idi's mother supposedly bewitched him, and he died.

Rumors claimed that Idi's mother was a witch doctor and could protect herself with her spells. In fact, Amin's home region is steeped in witchcraft and mystical beliefs. In an area where a rainstorm could be a lifesaver, people would sacrifice a goat or cow to the god of rain. Any misfortune, from a stillborn child to a failed crop, was attributed to the work of an angry god, a vengeful ancestor, or a sly enemy. Witch doctors provided medicines and charms to prevent these strokes of bad luck. Idi grew up believing in rituals, oracles, blood sacrifices, and potent enchantments.

When Idi was a boy, he and his mother moved often. In one village, he sold *mandazi*, or African doughnuts, beside the dirt roads that led to the army barracks. In another village, he learned his mother's language of Luganda and also Swahili. He spoke English with difficulty, however, and his education probably never advanced beyond the second grade. One observer recalled Idi as a large boy who liked to dominate the other children with his strength.

Career in the King's African Rifles

At age twenty, Idi was pleased to join the King's African Rifles—first as a kitchen worker, then as a private. He had grown into a huge man at six feet four inches and more than two hundred pounds. Amin loved the roughest sports, such as boxing and rugby, and for several years

Idi Amin joined the King's African Rifles, a unit of Ugandans in the British colonial forces, when he was twenty years old and rose steadily through the ranks.

in the 1950s was the heavyweight boxing champion of Uganda. A doctor for the amateur boxing association was shocked by Amin's killer instinct in the ring. The young Ugandan threw each punch with such ferocity that he seemed bent on killing his opponent, not simply defeating him.

Amin enjoyed army life from the beginning. Crude and easygoing, he often entertained his fellow soldiers with jokes and pranks. At about this time he became a Muslim, the religion he followed throughout his adult life. He was like other Nubians, or "Nubis"—career soldiers, mostly Muslims, who stocked the lower ranks of the British army in east Africa. In the opinion of George Ivan Smith, a United Nations diplomat in Africa, Amin's loyalties were set in stone very early. "He considered himself first and foremost a Nubian/Kakwa, secondly a Muslim, thirdly a west Niler, and fourthly a Ugandan."[1]

As a soldier, Amin was anxious to please his commanders. His boots were always polished, his uniform starched and spotless. He was willing to obey orders without question, and was not squeamish about using violence. He was also willing to falsify his military exploits. Amin often claimed to have fought alongside British forces in Burma in World War II, but this was a lie. His first important military action was to fight the Mau Mau,

When the King's African Rifles fought the Mau Mau (pictured), a terrorist group that fought to end British rule in Kenya, Amin became known for his excessive cruelty.

a terrorist group who tried to end British rule in Kenya in the early 1950s. Stories arose about Amin's ruthless treatment of the rebels. KAR troops killed one Mau Mau general and for days paraded his body around the local villages.

Despite his illiteracy, Amin rose steadily in the ranks of the Ugandan army. He was proud to be one of only two native Ugandan soldiers commissioned as officers before independence. This achievement won him a certain notoriety among native Ugandans.

Amin soon revealed a streak of murderous cruelty. In 1962, he was ordered to stop cattle rustling between the Karimojong and Pokot tribes. These were native herdsmen who raided each other's livestock almost as much for sport as profit. Despite orders merely to disarm the rustlers, Amin chose a more brutal solution. His platoon shot dozens of Pokot herdsmen and left them to be devoured by hyenas. He used torture and mutilation to force the Karimojong to surrender their weapons.

Actions like these brought protests from members of Obote's government. Uganda's British-born governor, Sir Walter Couts, demanded that the military chief be prosecuted. Obote, however, feared that such a move would cause a backlash from the army and the people. Amin was a bold, raucous, colorful soldier. As a native Ugandan who had achieved officer status, he held the admiration of many inside and outside the military. Obote gave him a severe reprimand, but nothing more. Couts, however, had no doubts about Amin's character. "I warn you," he told Obote, "this officer could cause you trouble in the future."[2]

For his part, Amin despised the younger men who had gone to military college before joining the Ugandan army. He often complained to his commander about their arrogance and lack of discipline. He suspected it was they who spread stories that accused him of cowardice in battle. Eventually, Amin began to train his own troops from among the Kakwa. Should trouble arise, he would be ready. A split was developing between soldiers loyal to Obote and those loyal to Amin.

Obote's Coup d'état

Obote recognized that Idi Amin, as an officer with a large following, would be a valuable asset. Obote gave Amin rapid promotions. Finally Amin took command of all of Uganda's military forces. Amin's loyalty enabled him to become Obote's protégé and ally, his right-hand man.

Amin wasted no time before he used his new position for personal gain. With Obote's approval, he smuggled weapons to rebels trying to topple the government of Uganda's neighbor, the Belgian Congo. In return for the weapons, Amin received hoards of ivory and gold seized from villages that the rebels had held. Since no records

Sir Walter Couts (right), the British-born governor of Uganda, warned Prime Minister Obote (left) that Amin would cause trouble for Obote in the future.

21

were kept of these deals, Amin was able to reward himself handsomely. He began to deposit huge sums in the bank at Kampala, the Ugandan capital. About this episode, Henry Kyemba, an official in Obote's government, wrote: "To me, [Amin] was always charming and easy to work with, but he also displayed a ruthless practicality, individuality and enterprise. For the first time I saw the effects of his particular intelligence which enabled him to snatch any advantage unconsciously offered and turn it to his own benefit."[3]

Amin enjoyed flaunting his new power and wealth. For a friend who was about to be married, he laughed and pulled an enormous stack of bills from his pocket as a

In 1962, Ugandans celebrated their complete independence from Great Britain, not knowing that their country would soon be under the control of a brutal dictator.

22

IDI AMIN

wedding present. At one point, Amin brazenly tried to deposit a gold bar in his bank account, which not only revealed the secret Congolese operation but also sparked accusations of corruption against Obote's government.

With Amin's army on his side, Obote shrugged off the charges. Yet while Obote was away on an official trip in the north, Uganda's lawmakers took a bold action. They passed a vote of no confidence to end Obote's elected term. Instead of resigning, Obote ordered Amin to lead a coup d'état, or revolt against the government. Obote's opponents had the rule of law on their side, but they lacked military force of any kind. The coup was successful. Obote passed a new constitution, with himself as president. He also declared martial law, or law enforced by the army, to stifle any further opposition. Political rivals were imprisoned without trial. At a single stroke, Obote had tightened his grip on the country. This meant that Amin, who enjoyed Obote's trust, could do as he liked as military commander.

CHAPTER 2

AMIN TAKES CONTROL

Milton Obote increasingly clamped down on the people's freedoms in Uganda. His new constitution abolished the four kingdoms. Instead, Uganda was divided into four districts controlled by the military. Buganda's King Freddie protested bitterly, but Obote no longer feared his influence.

In May 1966, Obote embarrassed King Freddie when he arrested several of his closest aides. Outraged, the Baganda tribe erupted. King Freddie's people barricaded the road that led to Kampala from the king's palace outside town. They threw stones and bricks at police cars and military vehicles. Fears arose that Milton Obote might be forced to abandon his own capital city.

Obote decided that the crisis called for military force. He ordered Amin and his troops to assault the Buganda palace and arrest King Freddie. By the time Amin launched the attack, the palace compound was filled with armed supporters of the king. They put up an unexpectedly strong fight. Amin, obviously enjoying himself, raced to Obote's compound in an open jeep equipped with a six-foot gun. He wanted permission to shell the king's compound. Obote agreed, and minutes later two shells exploded into the palace walls. Hundreds were killed in the ensuing battle. A heavy thunderstorm slowed the troops' progress enough for King Freddie to escape. Amin and his men spent the next few days looting the ornate palace. With a huge smile, Amin returned to give Obote some trophies: King Freddie's presidential flag and a special cap

After King Freddie (pictured) managed to escape Amin's attack on his palace compound, he left Uganda for England.

he had worn as ceremonial chief of the armed forces. As for the king, he managed leave Uganda for London, England, where he died in 1969.

Amin's Wives

Leading the assault on King Freddie's palace made Idi Amin even more of a national figure in Uganda. People talked about this brazen commander as if he were a fictional character. From his boxing championships to his habit of being caught in scandals, he was colorful and unpredictable. His decision to get married also managed to raise eyebrows.

Amin met his first wife, Malyamu Kibedi, when he was a soldier in the King's African Rifles. Although she and Amin had several children, they were not formally married until 1966. Soon after his marriage to Malyamu, Amin decided to take another wife. Islamic law allows a husband to have several wives, and usually all the wives live together in the same house. Marrying two women almost at once, however, was very unusual even among the Muslims of Uganda. Amin's second wife, Kay Adroa, had comforted him during the scandal about his deposits of gold bars. She was the daughter of a clergyman and had a college education. Quiet and dignified, she seemed an odd match for the talkative, aggressive commander.

Under Islamic law, men are allowed to have several wives. Amin, pictured in this 1979 photo with twenty-three of his children, had at least five wives.

Less than a year later, Amin married yet again, this time to a woman who was a member of the Langi, Obote's tribe. Onlookers saw this marriage as a transparent attempt by Amin to show Obote that tribal differences should not come between them. By the late 1960s, Amin, who was often described as an overgrown child, had fifteen children of his own. With his military rank, he and his family lived in a style that few Ugandans could afford.

Steps Toward a Showdown

For ordinary citizens, the country seemed to decline month by month. Corruption was rife, with people desperately buying favors from soldiers, police officers, and government officials. In 1969, Obote outlawed all political parties. He jailed hundreds of his political opponents without trial. To win back the people's support, Obote offered a plan called the "Common Man's Charter," intended to update the Ugandan government and eliminate the remains of British colonial policies. The majority of Ugandans were not impressed. Much of their anger was focused on businesspeople, particularly Asians, whose capital investments Obote was anxious to preserve.

The people called "Asians" in Uganda were actually Hindus and Muslims from India and Pakistan. Some Asian families had arrived in Uganda early in the twentieth century. They worked as merchants and civil servants in the British protectorate government. Later came Asians who were educated in law, medicine, and engineering, or who set up large trading companies in sugar, coffee, cotton, and other commodities. Asians played a vital part in Uganda's economy and also reaped many of its rewards. Signs of their wealth had long caused hostility among native Ugandans. Obote, who knew the importance of the Asians, was included in the angry tide.

In December 1969, resentment against Obote burst into violence. At a political meeting in Kampala, Obote was shot in the jaw by a would-be assassin. Miraculously, he survived. Amin was not at the meeting, and some members of the government immediately suspected him of planning the attempt on Obote's life. From his hospital bed, Obote wrote orders that Amin should be told about the shooting. Soldiers rushed to Amin's compound less than a mile from the meeting hall. When Amin saw the soldiers, he fled by vaulting over a barbed-wire fence in bare feet. It was hours before he reappeared. He explained that he feared a coup had taken place and that the soldiers had come to arrest him.

A month later, the army's second-in-command, Brigadier Pierino Okoya, accused Amin of desertion and cowardice for his actions after the assassination attempt. Amin fumed, but said little. A few days afterward, Okoya and his wife were found shot to death in Okoya's hometown. Although Amin was the prime suspect, he was able to block all inquiries by ordering his soldiers to remain silent. No charges were ever brought in the case.

What had been a hidden struggle was emerging into the open. Amin knew that his power had increased to a level that made him a threat to Obote. In his years of supporting Congolese rebels, Amin had recruited many southern Sudanese soldiers who lived not far from his home West Nile district.

Their language and customs had much in common with Amin's native Kakwa tribe, and many shared Amin's Muslim faith. Amin promised to support them in a civil war against the Sudan government in exchange for their loyalty to him. Amin's personal soldiers occupied every level of the military. In turn, Obote had organized elite groups of Langi soldiers who would fight for him. Above all, Idi Amin was unpredictable. Obote intended to prepare for anything.

Amin Leads a Coup

In January 1971, Milton Obote traveled to Singapore to attend a conference. While he was there, he received

When Amin (at wheel of jeep) staged a military coup and seized control of the country, Ugandans welcomed him as a liberator who freed them from Obote's hated government.

reports from his ministers in Kampala that another plot to assassinate him was in the works. Obote sent orders to arrest Amin and two cabinet ministers who were suspected of joining the plot.

Amin heard about the orders from his own contacts in the government. He recognized the chance presented by Obote's absence from the country and Obote supporters being unprepared for a decisive grab for power. Amin knew he had to act quickly. Early in the afternoon on January 24, he called his most trusted officers and told them to take control of the armories, where weapons and ammunition were stored. They also commandeered several tanks and the national radio station. Within hours, Amin had gathered soldiers who were loyal to him from all over the country. They sealed off the airport at Entebbe and surrounded Obote's compound. Tanks and soldiers filled the streets of Kampala. The military coup was a success.

The next day, a triumphant Amin appeared in public to announce his takeover of Uganda. "I am not a politician but a professional soldier," he declared to the people. "I am therefore a man of few words and I have been brief throughout my professional career."[4] Observers noted that Amin made speech after speech throughout Uganda in which he explained how little he enjoyed speaking.

Amin took the oath of office on January 6, 1971. Ugandans hoped that the new president would bring democracy to their country.

Drums pounded and fiddles played as crowds in Kampala cheered their new leader. Amin, already popular as a native officer who had risen to the top, was viewed by many as a liberator. Obote's hated government was gone, and people hoped that a fresh start under Amin would place Uganda back on the path to democracy and freedom.

In Singapore, Obote was unable to get news about the situation in Uganda. He called his minister of internal affairs in Kampala to see if Amin had been arrested as ordered, but the call did not go through. Obote was on a plane bound for Nairobi, Kenya, when his aides heard radio reports that his government had been overthrown. At first, Obote hoped to return quickly to Uganda and organize an army made up of his supporters. He soon realized it was too late. Idi Amin had done the unexpected once more. His lightning takeover had shocked his opponents and left them helpless. Obote flew instead to Dar es Salaam in neighboring Tanzania. There he was welcomed by the sympathetic government as Uganda's leader in exile.

Celebrations and Ominous Signs

The first weeks of Idi Amin's rule were occupied mainly with celebrations and speeches. At this point, Amin had few concerns about running the country. It pleased him to travel about in full uniform, by car or helicopter, and stop at major towns to address the happy crowds. Since he could barely read, he avoided written speeches and

Crowds thronged around Amin when he traveled around Uganda. Amin's new government won support from Ugandans and from countries around the world.

spoke off the cuff. He would promise his listeners to deliver whatever they needed—a hospital, a playground, new housing. Afterward, he would remind his aides to make notes of his promises, but few were ever kept.

Amin's assistants were surprised at how lightly he approached the task of governing Uganda. Henry Kyemba, who had served under Obote, was allowed to join Amin's government as a minister in his cabinet, or group of advisers. When Kyemba returned to Kampala, the new leader's first question to him was, "What did you bring me from Singapore?" Amin was delighted that Kyemba had bought him a small radio and some cloth for his wife. More serious matters could wait.

Immediately after the coup, the members of the cabinet thought that Amin's lack of experience in state affairs might offer them a great opportunity to help him govern. At the first meetings, Amin was careful to show his willingness to listen to his ministers. He admitted he was no politician, and said he realized he needed their help to run the country. He took their advice and appointed people with experience and ideas. The various tribes were well represented in the new government, and there was a balance of Christians and Muslims.

A few signs, however, were more ominous. Amin insisted on making government officials part of the military. Each minister was sworn in as a civilian cadet and required to wear a uniform. Amin let them know that they were now subject to military discipline. Although he appointed only a few of his own people to the cabinet, one of them was a new minister of defense. A month after the coup, Amin announced on the radio that his military government would remain in control for at least five years. He rarely discussed military matters with cabinet members. Amin was, as he said, a professional soldier. He made it clear that the army was his area— and the army controlled the nation.

Acceptance for the New Regime

Amin's military takeover of Uganda seemed to go smoothly. Under the direction of his ministers, the country returned to work. In the world's eyes, the coup was

Because he was almost illiterate, Amin (far right) preferred not to use written speeches when he spoke at press conferences or any public venues.

generally seen in a positive light. Amin's new government was quickly recognized by many countries, including Israel, Great Britain, and the United States. These countries had been outraged when Obote had placed foreign-owned businesses under the control of Uganda's government. One of Amin's first decrees was to reverse Obote's takeover. Foreign businesspeople thought they could work with the new leader, if only because their assets had been restored.

Another reason Amin's new government won such quick support had to do with the politics of the region. Israel wanted Uganda to support the Sudanese rebels fighting against the Islamic government in southern Sudan. The Sudanese government was aligned with Israel's Arab foes, and any military action that kept their forces occupied was welcome to the Israelis. Obote had balked at Israel's plan, but Amin cheerfully agreed. As for Great Britain, it still sold weapons to the government of South Africa, whose racist system of white rule, called apartheid, was under fire all over Africa. Milton Obote had criticized these sales and threatened to lead a continent-wide boycott of South Africa. The British Foreign Office thought that Amin would cease these protests.

A British Foreign Office report on the situation said: "We now have a thoroughly pro-Western set-up in Uganda, of which we should take prompt advantage. Amin needs our help."[5] Amin himself was seen as "popular and a natural leader of men, but simple and practically illiterate."[6] From the outset, Amin took great pains to appear pro-British. He told one visiting Foreign Office minister that he greatly desired a signed portrait of Queen Elizabeth. He claimed to have dictated "a very nice letter" to the queen.

Wealthy Ugandan farmers and business owners from the dominant Baganda tribe also supported Amin. He had thrown out the hated Obote, who had exiled their tribal chief, and for that the new leader deserved their thanks. (They apparently had forgiven Amin for shelling King Freddie's compound.) Amin pleased them further when he released King Freddie's relatives from jail, where they had languished for five years. He even arranged for King Freddie's body to be returned from Great Britain so it could be reburied in Uganda.

What these supporters failed to realize was how determined Amin was to strengthen his grip on power. African leaders outside Uganda, such as Tanzania's president Julius Nyerere and Jomo Kenyatta of Kenya, had no such illusions. They were skeptical of Amin's military background and feared the worst.

A rebel himself, Amin imagined all sorts of plots against him. Obote's power base had been his tribespeople inside the military. These included people from Obote's tribe, the Langi, and a related group, the Acholi, who made up a large part of the army. Amin decided that none of them could be trusted. He had no qualms about using violence to preserve his position. As he smiled to the crowds, he was plotting the murder of his enemies.

Bloody Purges

The first killings took place on the night of the coup. In the officers' mess at the army barracks in Malire, Amin's soldiers cornered several officers known to be loyal to Obote. The officers were beaten to death with rifle butts and bottles. Another victim was the army chief of staff, Brigadier Suleiman Hussein. Obote had ordered Hussein to arrest Amin, but when the coup broke out, Hussein went into hiding. Days later, he was arrested himself and brought to Luzira Prison. Like the other officers, he was bludgeoned with rifle butts. One of Amin's servants declared that Hussein's head was delivered to Amin, who kept it in his own refrigerator. At night, Amin reportedly placed the head on his dining room table and scolded it for daring to oppose him.

Another killing site was Makindye Prison, an army facility. Joshua Wakholi, a former minister in Obote's government, was arrested and held in Makindye, next door to a cell called "Singapore." This was where condemned soldiers and civilians were taken. Wakholi described one night when a handful of Amin's troops shot and stabbed thirty-six officers and one corporal. The following morning, Wakholi and other prisoners were ordered to clean up the Singapore cell. The floor, Wakholi recalled, was covered in blood.

Incidents like this quickly multiplied. Amin was determined to eliminate his enemies in the military and the government. Amin ordered several hundred Langi soldiers to assemble at their barracks at Lira. As

Amin's soldiers captured and usually killed those suspected of being enemies of the regime. This photo shows soldiers as they prepare to execute a rebel.

soon as they arrived, his soldiers attacked them with bayonets and dumped the corpses into the Nile. Hundreds of Acholi and Langi soldiers were slaughtered at the

Malire, Mbarara, and Jinja barracks. When Obote supporters, both soldiers and civilians, tried to escape into neighboring Sudan, they were captured by Sudanese guerrillas in Amin's service. Uganda's new leader then calmly ordered their executions.

Foreign reporters were also caught in the violence. Early in July after the coup, two Americans began to investigate reports of massacres. One of them, a journalist named Nicholas Stroh, angered Major Juma Aiga, the second-ranked officer at the Mbarara barracks, with his probing questions. Stroh and his partner, university professor Robert Siedle, were killed and their bodies buried in shallow graves. When the American embassy began to investigate, the bodies were dug up and burned. Amin formed a commission led by a British judge to seek facts about the killings. When the inquiry accused the two commanding officers at Mbarara, Amin scoffed and said the commission was biased from the start. The judge, fearing for his life, fled Uganda. Amin rewarded the commander at Mbarara with a string of promotions.

Amin also took care to tie up loose ends from his years as Obote's military chief. Amin had escaped being officially implicated in the murders of Pierino Okoya and his wife. Now he ordered the deaths of a gang of *kondos*—Ugandan for "armed robbers"—who had

Barbarity and Cannibalism

Rarely were Amin's enemies simply killed. According to personnel in Uganda's hospitals, the bodies were usually mutilated in some way—eyes gouged out, noses and lips crushed, livers and other organs ripped out. Amin ordered his agents to engage in this behavior. Often Amin demanded that hospital staff leave him alone with the bodies of his victims, for what purpose he did not say. Henry Kyemba, Amin's minister of health, had his own suspicions, and they were shared by the people of Uganda. Idi Amin, they believed, had a taste for human blood.

Kyemba attributed Amin's behavior partly to his warped personality and partly to his tribal background. Amin's tribe, the Kakwa, were known to practice blood rituals on the dead bodies of their foes. In his book about Amin, *A State of Blood*, Kyemba writes:

> These involve cutting a piece of flesh from the body to subdue the dead man's spirit or tasting the victim's blood to render the spirit harmless—a spirit, it is believed, will not revenge itself on a body that has become in effect its own. Such rituals still exist among the Kakwa. If they kill a man, it is their practice to insert a knife in the body and touch the bloody blade to their lips.

Kyemba also heard Amin boast several times in private that he had eaten human flesh. Amin seemed to enjoy shocking his listeners with this admission. He declared that the practice was not unusual in his home district. Once in a conversation with a Ugandan doctor about various kinds of meat, Amin told him, "I have eaten human meat. It is very salty, even more salty than leopard meat."

Whatever the truth of these stories, they certainly added to Amin's sinister mystique. For many Ugandans, whether or not they believed in the old tribal superstitions, the stories of a ruler who had tasted the flesh of his enemies struck a deep chord of helpless fear.

Amin (in white uniform) had little knowledge of how to run the country, but liked to inspect his troops and travel around Uganda in full uniform.

carried out the killings for him. He then seized and executed the police officers who had investigated the case.

Law in Uganda became whatever Amin decreed it to be. Four months after the coup, Amin announced that any suspect could be held without a trial. He ordered his troops to shoot anyone suspected of having committed, or even planning to commit, a crime. The sound of gunfire grew commonplace around Uganda's cities.

The death sentences that Amin passed were delivered in code and slang. He could be almost lighthearted in his choice of words. Referring to a prisoner, he might say to an officer, "Give him the VIP treatment." This meant that the victim was to be tortured before being killed. "Take him to Malire," another popular phrase, meant the person should be moved to the military prison. Amin was also fond of the Nubian term *kalasi*, meaning "death." Unable to write, he conveyed all his orders verbally, in person or on the phone. Only a few of Amin's closest henchmen knew the extent of the purges. His method had the added benefit of avoiding any paper trail. In fact, the purge murders tended to increase in number when Amin was out of the country. He thought that he could, if necessary, deny any knowledge of the killings.

CHAPTER 3

THE EXPULSION OF THE ASIANS

Since military life was all he knew, Amin rapidly converted Uganda into a military state. He changed the name of Government House, where his offices were located, to "the Command Post." He transferred the powers of the civilian cabinet to his council of military advisers and installed military tribunals to replace civil courts. Army commanders across the country ran their territories like local warlords. Soldiers kept civilians in line with a constant threat of violence. Amin continued to lure troops from Sudan as well as from the Kakwa and other warrior tribes inside and outside Uganda. Almost daily, Sudanese recruits were trucked into Uganda with promises of the good life under General Amin. Eventually almost three-fourths of his army was foreign-born. Ugandans often felt like the victims of an occupation force.

Amin realized his power depended on the allegiance of these troops. The simplest way to keep their loyalty was to buy it. To do this, Amin knew he would need lots of cash and merchandise. Maintaining a flow of money to the military was the goal of his foreign policy, such as it was, from the beginning.

Amin lacked the most basic understanding of economics. The constraints of a traditional budget plan meant nothing to him. His minister of planning and economic development warned him about huge gaps between spending and revenues in his government. The worst offender was the ministry of defense, which after less than a year of Amin's rule was more than $10 million in the red. Under Amin, military spending in Uganda had risen threefold. Many of the expenditures were ludicrous—for example, Amin had decided to build a navy even though Uganda is a landlocked nation. When told that Uganda was almost bankrupt, Amin's reply was, "Well, print more money."[7]

The details of budget management bored Amin. His solution to the problem, as usual, was to take strong action. For the region and the world, it was the first true glimpse of the unpredictable man who led Uganda.

Gadhafi and the Break with Israel

Early in 1972, Amin was in West Germany discussing ways to tap Uganda's oil resources. He chanced to meet a delegation of Libyans in his hotel and decided to stop in Libya on his way home. Although Amin's personal airliner was Israeli-made and the pilot and crew were Israelis, he saw nothing wrong with paying a call on Libya's leader Muammar Gadhafi, who was virulently anti-Israel. Gadhafi quickly saw a chance to scuttle one of Israel's key relationships in Africa. He made a deal with Amin. Libya would provide Uganda with financial and military aid if Amin would cut all ties to the Israelis.

Such a radical switch in foreign policy was no problem for Idi Amin. Upon his return to Uganda, he immediately expelled all Israeli military advisers, including friends he had known since his paratroop training as a young soldier. Numerous Israeli-backed building projects were ended, and their managers sent home. To show his new scorn for Israel, Amin broadcast speeches that criticized Zionism, the idea that Israel should be a haven for Jews worldwide. He said that Israel should return Arab lands captured in a 1967 war. When Israel's diplomats protested,

Amin increased the intensity of his attacks. He declared that Israel should be wiped off the face of the earth. He even praised German Nazi leader Adolf Hitler for his success at killing Jews during the 1930s and 1940s.

Amin convinced Libya, the oil-rich nation of Saudi Arabia, and other Arab states to give Uganda money by emphasizing his background as a Muslim. (In truth, Amin believed just as much in fortune-telling and witchcraft). He even tried to convince Gadhafi and other Arab leaders that Uganda was a Muslim

Libya's leader Muammar Gadhafi promised financial and military aid to Uganda if Amin cut all ties with Israel.

nation. Amin exaggerated the number of Muslims in his country, as if they were in the majority instead of being only 6 percent of the population. He built mosques, published translations of the Koran, the Islamic holy book, into local languages, and bribed people to convert to Islam. He even began to build a large mosque in downtown Kampala, a project that was never completed.

In exchange, Gadhafi offered business and military support. A joint bank, the Libyan Arab Ugandan Bank for Foreign Trade and Development, was started in Kampala. Libyans helped to build two hospitals in Uganda and donated millions of dollars for other projects. Libya also took over the training of Ugandan troops, which Israel had done since Obote's regime. Gadhafi sent money from his fund for a holy war, called a jihad. The money would be used to eliminate what Gadhafi thought were Uganda's last few Christians and help turn Uganda into a Muslim state. Pleased with his new partnership, Amin swore he would use his army and air force to fight Israel and the Zionists.

Amin's Fateful Dream

Money from Libya, Saudi Arabia, and other Arab nations was helpful, but Amin needed more. He brooded on the problem. On August 5, 1972, the general called a meeting of his senior military advisers at the Government House in Kampala. Still in his pajamas, Amin announced that God had spoken to him in a dream the night before. God had ordered him to expel the Asian community from Uganda and take all their houses and businesses, including mills, breweries, cotton factories, sugar refineries, hotels, and shops. In other words, Amin's dream would become state policy. Once a journalist had asked him, "Do you have many visions?" Amin replied, "Only when necessary."[8] It was clear that Amin's dream was a deliberate attempt to justify what he planned to do anyway.

Most of the affluent middle class in Uganda was made up of Asians—Hindus and Muslims from India and Pakistan. They were factory owners, merchants, bureaucrats, and shopkeepers. Despite their economic success, the Asians had mixed uneasily with the general society in Uganda. They felt more comfortable with British rulers in Uganda than with the new generation of native leaders. In 1962, when Uganda became independent and blacks took power, many Asians planned to return to India or Pakistan. In fact, however, almost all of them stayed. They had grown fond of the natural

Hindus and Muslims from India and Pakistan made up most of Uganda's wealthy middle class. In 1972, Amin ordered all Asians to leave within three months.

beauty of the country as well as of the society they had made for themselves—a sort of "Little India." The hard-working Asians in Uganda were the backbone of the country's economy. At this point, despite Amin's failings as a leader, Uganda's economic activity was still robust. Removing the Asians would cause massive disruptions.

Nevertheless, Amin went forward with the expulsion order. In a decree read on Radio Uganda, he declared that all Asians, numbering some sixty thousand or more, must leave Uganda within ninety days. He called it his "economic war." A scowling Amin met with leaders of the Asian community to affirm his plan. The Asian leaders could not believe the news reports. They recalled how their people had linked arms with blacks and whites and danced in the streets of Kampala when Amin had overthrown Obote. They hoped to reason with the general, but instead they were met with a torrent of abuse. "You have milked the Ugandan cow without feeding it,"[9] he told them. He claimed that they had stolen from the economy by sending their profits to their relatives in India and Great Britain. Now the tables would be turned. The Asian community was hated by all native Ugandans, he said, and thus the Asians must leave by November 9. "If you don't go by then," he told them, "I will make you feel as if you are sitting on fire."[10]

The Plan Proceeds

Many ordinary Ugandans were shocked by the news but basically supported the decree. Black Ugandans felt that Asians had been handed all the plum positions by the British and now were using their economic power to exploit blacks. Jokes about Asian shopkeepers cheating their customers were commonplace. Asians supposedly loved to flaunt their wealth, particularly their automobiles, which few black Ugandans could afford. While blacks were just starting to learn

As the deadline for them to leave Uganda drew closer, Asians clamored for vouchers that would allow them to relocate to England.

about Amin's murderous regime (many had relatives missing and believed dead), they still blamed the chaos in their country on the Asians. Some blacks suspected that Amin, under pressure from Britain or the United States, would finally back down on his order before

November 9. Still, when the countdown number was updated each day on the evening news, many black Ugandans cheered.

Great Britain rushed to persuade Amin to change his decision. If expelled, most of the Asians planned to take advantage of their British passports and relocate in England. Members of Parliament hoped to avoid a sudden flood of jobless foreigners into their country. A British diplomat flew to Kampala to meet with Amin, but the general kept him waiting for four days. Amin was worried that his weak command of English would be embarrassing in face-to-face negotiations. The two did finally meet, but nothing was accomplished.

Finally, a British military officer tried to reason with the ruler. Lieutenant Colonel Ian Grahame had served in Uganda for more than fifteen years, and Amin considered him his closest friend. British officers like Grahame were among the few people for whom the former soldier Amin had genuine respect. Grahame spoke bluntly to Amin about how unfair his Asian plan was and how it could wreck Uganda. Afterward, Amin softened some aspects of the expulsion. Asians who had become Ugandan citizens could stay. When Amin appeared on Ugandan television a few days later, however, he reversed himself. All the Asian "bloodsuckers" must leave, he said, with no exceptions. Those who remained after the deadline would be put in detention camps.

The Economy Collapses

As the deadline approached, Asians scrambled to make preparations. They waited in lines all over Kampala—for shots, for passports, and for small cash allowances, about one hundred dollars per family. Each Asian family was allowed only two suitcases of personal items. They had to abandon their houses, furniture, cars, and appliances. Hundreds of Asians piled into trains, dubbed "Kampala Specials," bound for East African coastal cities such as Mombasa and Dar es Salaam. Amin's police set up roadblocks on the streets to the airport in order to steal the Asians' most valuable items. The airport became more crowded each day. By October 1972, there were thirty

Each Asian family was allowed to take only two suitcases and about one hundred dollars with them when they left Uganda.

flights a week from Kampala to London. Boxes of goods piled up on the runways, intended for mailing to England. Eventually, army officers cut open the boxes and took what they wanted. Some days Amin himself appeared at the airport in full uniform to laugh at the departing Asians. "This is wonderful," he told his men, "wonderful."[11]

In December, Amin began the process of doling out the Asians' property. He gave his favorite officers hotels, shops, farms, and factories to do with as they pleased. A photograph from this period shows Amin striding down a street in Kampala with several officers and a clerk with a notebook. He is in the act of giving away shops and businesses. There was no plan, just spur-of-the-moment decisions. Committees were formed to speed the process, but their work was just as haphazard.

Not surprisingly, the officers and soldiers who took over lacked the first idea of how to run these businesses. Many invited members of their families or tribes to take items off the shelves. They did not know how to order new stock or even how much to charge for the merchandise. Sometimes the new owner would ask customers how much they paid for an item the last time. One soldier who was given a clothing store mistook the collar size of shirts for their price. Pharmacy owners sold dangerous drugs that they knew nothing about. Medical equipment was ripped

After the Asians left, Amin gave their shops and businesses to his favorite soldiers and officers even though they knew nothing about running those businesses. The Ugandan economy quickly collapsed.

out of doctors' offices and sold. Prices changed wildly from day to day.

Some officers became fabulously wealthy overnight, with several houses and a fleet of cars. Overall, however, the expulsion and its results dealt a death blow to Uganda's economy. Items such as sugar, butter, salt, tea, and bread became scarce, then disappeared entirely. Dairy cows were slaughtered for meat, and the dairy industry collapsed. A black market arose that sold the most basic consumer goods for enormous prices.

Amin was puzzled by the economic collapse. He had assumed that farms and businesses practically ran themselves. In desperation, he would seize a failing company from one inept owner and give it to another. Fearful of losing a chance at wealth, the new owner would sell everything as quickly as possible and pocket the cash. As things continued to decline, Amin ordered his ministers to blame the whole mess on the Asians' system of doing business. The wealth of Uganda drained away in a matter of months.

CHAPTER 4

CLOWN AND TYRANT

In September 1972, exiled former president Milton Obote launched an invasion of Uganda from Tanzania on the southern border. Obote's forces numbered no more than one thousand, they were badly equipped, and they lacked a good plan. They counted on Ugandans to rise up against Amin and do much of their work for them. The people, however, were told via radio reports that the invaders were Tanzanian forces and gave them no support. Obote's men also hoped to take Entebbe airport with a lightning guerrilla raid, but their aircraft stalled, and the raid never happened. Overall, the coup attempt was a miserable failure. Amin's army repelled it easily, and Amin himself quickly saw an opportunity to use the invasion for his own purposes.

Ugandan TV and radio greatly exaggerated the extent of the invasion. Reports said that Obote's guerrillas had taken over several towns throughout Uganda. Amin continued to tell the people that Tanzania was behind the invasion, even though that country had only allowed the rebels to train there. The general also hinted that Great Britain and Israel were involved. When news of the invasion's failure finally came out, it was presented as a great victory for Idi Amin and his invincible army.

This event set the stage for years of oppression in Uganda. Amin used the invasion as an excuse to extend his killing spree to the general population. The invasion had conveniently shown that no one could be trusted, and no one would be allowed to criticize his rule.

When Obote's attempted coup failed, Amin first claimed it as a great victory for him and his army and then became even more cruel and violent toward the general population.

THE PSYCHOLOGY OF A DICTATOR

Some psychologists attribute Amin's mood swings to hypomania, a form of manic depression.

Many who have met Idi Amin Dada have remarked on his warmth and friendliness in face-to-face encounters. He seems playful and loves to joke and tease. Yet Amin could change at a moment's notice to a brutal killer, ready to eliminate even a friend to protect himself. Observing this capacity in Amin, some psychologists have tried to diagnose his particular form of psychosis, or mental illness.

One medical observer attributes his wild mood swings to a form of manic depression called hypomania. People with this disorder are active all the time, talk constantly, and sleep very little. They tend to jump from one idea to another with no connections that others can follow. Plans are based on impulse, with no apparent logic or purpose. Amin's ministers grew used to his calls after midnight when he would tell them excitedly about some new idea of his. The next day, more often than not, the plan was entirely forgotten. Bursts of such wild activity are followed by quiet periods, when the individual seems tired and depressed. Throughout his rule, Amin made regular visits to Mulago Hospital for days of rest.

Hypomania can also result in uncontrollable fits of anger. In such a fit, the person might be capable of anything. Reports indicate that Amin ordered many executions when he lost his temper. Like a child, he would lash out when he felt thwarted or cornered.

Another factor in Amin's mental makeup is the insecurity he felt as a child. He was a poor urchin dragged from place to place, then left to fend for himself around the military barracks. Observers believe he was motivated to make up for his rootless background, to prove himself as good as or better than anyone else again and again.

None of these diagnoses relieves Amin of ultimate responsibility for his crimes. Many have noted his apparent lack of any conscience or sense of pity for other human beings. These deficiencies have to do, above all, with personal character.

The Colorful Dictator

Within this swirl of activity, Amin still found time to announce his fourth marriage, this one to a dancer named Medina. She was part of a troupe of dancers that accompanied Amin on his speaking tours around the country. It pleased Amin to slip the news of his wedding into media reports of Obote's invasion. He even claimed, falsely of course, that Medina had been a gift from the Baganda thanking him for his support since the 1971 coup.

Entrenched in power now, Amin grew more eccentric each day. He had begun his military career as a disciplined soldier, albeit one with a dangerous streak of cruelty and violence. Now his discipline sagged into self-indulgence and personal whims. If Uganda was a prison and a slaughterhouse for others, for Amin it was a playhouse. There was, of course, no one to tell him no.

One example was his attitude toward money. To him, there was no difference between government spending and his own spending. He moved from one lavish house to another, and each one was equipped with expensive food, wines, clothing, furniture, electronics, cars, and whatever else he wanted. One of his cabinet ministers, Henry Kyemba, recalled how Amin maintained his cash supply. Ugandan law provided that small amounts of cash could be spent to gather intelligence. It was Amin's favorite provision. When he wanted money, he would tell Kyemba to get the funds from the treasury for some imaginary intelligence mission. The amounts began in the hundreds of dollars and rapidly rose to tens of thousands. The general's pockets always bulged with cash. He enjoyed giving it away in the streets for fun.

Amin also indulged his fondness for military pomp and pageantry. At public events, he would appear in full military uniform, based on the ones British officers wore. There were so many medals attached to the jacket that the cloth threatened to tear from the weight. Amin loved medals, although his were all self-awarded. Among his medals were the Victorious Cross (he was denied a copy of the Victoria Cross), Distinguished Service Order, Military Cross, and the CBE (Conqueror of the British Empire). He also liked kilts and bagpipes, and proclaimed himself the king of Scotland. At military parades, he would watch from a reviewing stand as his war toys passed in procession. The tanks and artillery guns were so heavy that they buckled the pavement in downtown Kampala.

To make up for his lack of education, Amin awarded himself all kinds of degrees and academic honors. He served as chancellor at Makerere University, gave himself a doctorate degree, and was the head of the political

Amin made four British businessmen carry him to a reception on a makeshift throne to demonstrate his authority over the British.

science department—all this despite barely being able to read and write.

Amin particularly enjoyed humiliating certain people to display his authority. Photographs show him in a sedan chair being carried on the shoulders of four British businessmen. When British residents in Kampala took an oath as army reserves, Amin forced them to kneel to him for the ceremony.

Amin and World Leaders

Amin also was anxious to show his prestige on the world stage. He wanted to be seen as a legitimate leader, the equal of other leaders in the world. Just as he never stopped talking at home in live speeches and broadcasts, he also sent a constant stream of letters and telegrams to other heads of state. The messages ranged from polite greetings to bizarre advice.

Amin claimed a special affection for Great Britain and Queen Elizabeth. Soon after he took power, he sent the queen a message of greeting. He kept photographs of her in his various offices and homes. He dictated a cable to the American president Richard Nixon. "You are one of the most brilliant leaders in the Western world and my best friend," Amin said. "I offer the advice that you should not again get involved militarily in Vietnam to assist the solution of the problems between north and south."[12] The United States cut aid to Uganda after Amin expelled the Asians. This resulted in another message: "My dear brother, it is quite true that you have enough problems on your plate [referring to the Watergate scandal] and it is surprising that you have the zeal to add fresh ones. . . . I ask Almighty God to help solve your problems."[13] In a cable to Tanzanian president Julius Nyerere, Amin swore that he had great respect for Nyerere and would marry him despite his graying hair.

Amin spoke freely to reporters when in the mood. Usually he tried to embarrass an enemy or rival. Referring to the Arabs' war against Israel, Amin said that the Israeli prime minister Golda Meir had only one choice: "to tuck up her knickers and run away in the direction of New York and Washington."[14]

A Documentary Film

More of Amin's odd behavior was on display in a 1974 documentary about him. Amin allowed French director Barbet Schroeder to film his activities in and around Kampala. The general is

Although Amin wanted the world to see him as a legitimate leader, his efforts to embarrass rivals like Israel's prime minister Golda Meir (pictured) made that unlikely.

shown observing military exercises, leading a cabinet meeting, shooing crocodiles on a river cruise, and playing the accordion at a dance. He talks and laughs throughout the film, and seems comfortable in front of the camera. Several times Amin insists that the people love him because he speaks the truth to them. When Schroeder asks him about the economy in Uganda, Amin says, "We are not following any policy at all."[15] Reminded about comments he made that Hitler did not kill enough Jews, Amin simply chuckles.

In the film, Schroeder included scenes of public executions in Amin's Uganda. Amin demanded that these scenes be cut, but Schroeder at first refused. Amin then arrested 150 French citizens in Uganda and threatened to kill them unless Schroeder changed the film. The director agreed. The original version of the film was not seen publicly until after Amin's fall from power.

This was typical Amin—chatting cheerfully one moment, then ordering someone's execution the next. Even so, his clownish behavior convinced many observers in the West to dismiss him as a harmless fool. With his

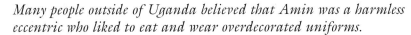

Many people outside of Uganda believed that Amin was a harmless eccentric who liked to eat and wear overdecorated uniforms.

ample stomach and his overdecorated uniform, he looked like a caricature of an African dictator. Some observers, however, saw through his act. Godfrey Lule, former minister of justice in Uganda, knew the reality of Amin's two-faced treachery. "For too long Amin has been considered a clown," Lule wrote. "Indeed, he is a clown, when he chooses. Face to face, he is relaxed, simple and charming—he seems incapable of wrongdoing or of sanctioning any crime. But this is no more than a façade. He is at heart a manipulator—charm and generosity are his two greatest weapons."[16]

Amin's Security Police

Whatever charm Amin had was wearing thin on the beleaguered people of Uganda. The economy was sinking into chaos, and ordinary citizens were beginning to learn the truth about the new regime. Amin was hopeless as an administrator. He was slaughtering his enemies to stay in power. What wealth remained was being given to Amin's officers and soldiers. Uganda's finest minds—doctors, engineers, business people—were fleeing the country. As people questioned his ability to lead, Amin relied on various arms of his security police to control them with terror. Amin set up three overlapping groups to handle arrests and monitor both citizens and soldiers. The groups were the military police unit, the Public Safety Unit, and the State Research Bureau.

Under Obote, the military police had enforced discipline among soldiers. Late in 1971, Major Hussein Marella, a Nubian, took control of Makindye Prison and made the military police into a feared unit. In *A State of Blood*, Henry Kyemba describes Marella as "one of the most vicious men I have ever met."[17] Under Marella, the military police extended its authority to civilians as well as military personnel. MPs, like members of the other units, were free to shoot suspects on the street.

Also in late 1971, a Nubian named Ali Towelli took over the public safety unit. This unit's headquarters was located at Naguru, three miles from the center of Kampala. The public safety unit began as part of the ordinary police force to combat armed robbery, which was frequent after the coup. It soon grew into a special force that rooted out Amin's supposed enemies all over the country. The public safety unit headquarters stood next to a high-rise training center and other tall buildings. From their windows, civil servants and secretaries could watch the firing squads execute prisoners. Motorists on nearby roads could hear the victims' cries. These public displays were intentional, to keep Ugandans in a state of fear and uncertainty.

As the number of killings increased, Towelli sought ways to save on bullets. He came up with a fiendish solution. As one prisoner awaited execution, a second one would be handed a sledgehammer, promised a reprieve, and forced to batter the first to death. A third prisoner was then brought from the cells with the same promise, and so forth.

The State Research Bureau

As brutal as the activities of the Public Safety Unit were, the most powerful and most frightening of Amin's security groups was the State Research Bureau, or secret police. Like the other groups, it was commanded by a loyal Nubian, Major Farouk Minawa. The State Research Bureau began as a military intelligence unit under Obote, but Amin made its agents his personal bodyguards. The three-story bureau headquarters was located next door to the President's Lodge on Nakasero Hill—a name that still fills Ugandans with dread. The headquarters building was the scene of countless murders during Amin's regime. An underground tunnel connected the structure with the President's Lodge and gave Amin a passage for a quick escape or to send victims to their deaths.

The two thousand agents of the State Research Bureau were the elite cogs in General Idi Amin's killing machine. Although they received salaries like other employees, most became wealthy by stealing money and goods from their victims. They also could earn fabulous sums by providing leads about Amin's enemies. Amin found it easy to recruit new members from among the poor Kakwa and southern Sudanese youths in the north-west. Instead of uniforms, the agents wore flowered shirts, bellbottom pants, and dark glasses. They drove brand-new black cars and frequently traveled on

As his country sank into economic chaos, people questioned Amin's ability to lead. In response, Amin used his security force to control Ugandans with terror.

overseas missions. There were almost no rules to restrict their behavior. They would capture and beat their victims brazenly in broad daylight.

The Murders Increase

The deadly work of Idi Amin's security units eventually took on its own crazy logic. To cover up a murder, lies had to be told. Those who knew they were lies then had to be eliminated, which resulted in more lies and more killings. Amin discovered new enemies and new threats to himself almost daily. He became obsessed with assassination attempts. He summed up his fears by saying, "No one can run faster than a bullet."[18]

Beginning with Obote's supporters in the army, Amin's circle of death widened to include cabinet members, judges, physicians, ambassadors, businesspeople, and even church officials. Thousands upon thousands of ordinary, innocent Ugandans also lost their lives in Amin's prisons and interrogation cells. Often the so-called offense had nothing to do with politics. Citizens were murdered for their cars or their girlfriends. The wrong word spoken to a soldier or agent could be fatal.

No trace remained of a typical system of justice. Local police officers had no authority whatsoever. If a family tried to report a son's disappearance, they were advised by the police to keep quiet about it. Anyone who complained to a security agent or one of Amin's soldiers was as good as dead. Once arrested, a person had no right to see his or her family or speak to a lawyer. Sentencing was done with a club, a hammer, or the barrel of a gun.

Fear made the people passive and cautious. Corpses sometimes lay on dirt roads for days, since showing concern for the dead might result in one's own murder. When it became impossible for Amin's thugs to bury all their victims, they began to dump truckloads of bodies in the Nile River, dozens of them every day. It was hoped that crocodiles would dispose of all the evidence, but motorists and fishermen in the area could attest that that did not happen. They kept their stories, however, to themselves.

CHAPTER 5

THE ENTEBBE RAID

In 1974, Libya's colonel Muammar Gadhafi flew to Uganda for a three-day visit. Amin greeted Gadhafi with an army guard of honor made up of Ugandan commandos who had trained in Libya. Gadhafi was there to help dedicate the new terminal building at Entebbe International Airport. It was a $10 million project, and the cost was shared by the two countries in a spirit of cooperation. Gadhafi also announced a gift of several MiG fighter planes. Amin was delighted.

Since 1972, when his relationship with Libya began, Amin had aligned himself with the most radical Arab nations and groups. One of these groups was the Palestine Liberation Organization, or PLO. The PLO was dedicated to removing Israelis from the land of Palestine, which had become, under a United Nations agreement in 1948, the nation of Israel. Gadhafi was a strong supporter of the PLO. His visit to Uganda and his gifts of money, military advisers, and weapons showed that he considered Idi Amin a partner in the Arab cause. Amin, in turn, was anxious to demonstrate his support for the PLO.

In 1975, Amin made a push to gain more friends for his regime. He made a cooperation agreement with the PLO. In July, Uganda hosted the summit conference of the Organization of African Unity (OAU), a group of African nations. The members even elected Amin their president. For Idi Amin to win this position despite his terrible violations of human rights troubled many

Amin built a strong relationship with radical Arab nations and groups. As president of the Organization of African Unity, Amin supported Arab interests in the Middle East.

observers. In protest, Tanzania's president Julius Nyerere and Zambia's leader Kenneth Kaunda boycotted the meetings. Amin showed his irritation by inviting Nyerere's top political opponent to attend instead.

Amin used his position as leader of the OAU to focus on conflicts in the Middle East. His pro-Arab rhetoric became even more pronounced. Overall, Amin built up his standing in the Arab world.

The Hijacking of Flight 139

That standing seemed to increase during a crisis in 1976. On June 27, Air France Flight 139 took off from Athens bound for Tel Aviv, Israel. Among the 246 passengers were 107 Israelis. In the air, the plane was hijacked by a group of four terrorists. Two of the terrorists were from the Popular Front for the Liberation of Palestine, and two were from a West German group. The plane first diverted to Tripoli, Libya, to refuel. Then, with the permission of Idi Amin, the plane landed at Entebbe Airport the next day. Three more terrorists joined the group in Uganda.

Henry Kyemba, the Ugandan minister of health, recalls that Amin telephoned him and was enthusiastic about the hijacking. He told Kyemba to gather a small medical team and meet him at the airport. Under international law, Amin should have treated the hijackers as criminals. Instead, he made a speech at the airport to express support for them and their cause. He then provided them with extra troops and weapons.

The hostages were taken to the old airport building, which was now a storehouse with broken windows, peeling paint, and rusted plumbing. There the hijackers, armed with pistols and grenades, separated the Jews from the other passengers. They demanded that Israel release more than fifty convicted terrorists from its prisons. If they were not released, the hijackers would begin to execute the Israeli hostages. On July 1, all the non-Israeli passengers were set free. The airplane's crew were also offered the chance to leave, but they chose to stay with the Israeli hostages.

Kyemba had no doubt that Amin was in on the plan. "The whole operation was being supervised by Amin himself," Kyemba wrote, "working together with the Palestinians based in Kampala. He thought he saw a fine opportunity to humiliate the Israelis and increase his stock with the Arabs. He wanted all the glory. 'Well, Kyemba,' he said to me several times, 'now I've got these people where I want them,' and 'I've got the Israelis fixed up this time.'"[19]

Behind the scenes, Israeli officials were in contact with their former ally, Amin. Retired colonel Burka Bar-Lev

IDI AMIN

phoned his old friend and used flattery and jokes to extract bits of information about the hostages. Meanwhile, the Israelis were discussing ways to rescue the prisoners.

The Raid on Entebbe

The hijackers' original deadline was moved back to July 4, mainly to accommodate Amin, who had flown to Mauritius to pass on his chairmanship at the Organization of African Unity annual summit. Amin had been looking forward to this event, and also he did not want observers to think he was afraid to leave Uganda during a crisis. Amin felt lighthearted on his trip. He was certain that Israel would have to bow to the hijackers' demands. The world would see how much influence Idi Amin had in the region. Unknown to Amin, however, the extended deadline also helped the Israelis develop a rescue plan.

Kyemba kept Amin updated on the condition of the hostages. Several became ill, and several others seemed to be faking illness in hopes of being moved to a hospital. On July 2, an elderly hostage named Dora Bloch choked on a piece of meat that had lodged in her throat. Bloch, who had joint British-Israeli citizenship, was rushed to Mulago Hospital in Kampala. The piece of meat was removed in a brief operation. Because of Bloch's age, Kyemba saw that she remained in the hospital and rested. Shortly afterward, Amin told Kyemba to return Bloch to the airport before the deadline arrived.

Amin arrived back at Entebbe early in the evening on July 3. He immediately visited the Israeli hostages, then retired to one of his compounds. Just after midnight on July 4, Amin received shocking news from the Entebbe airport. There was fighting at the airport, and it had been captured. The situation was confused and dangerous. It was unclear who had launched the attack. Amin assumed at first that Kenya or Tanzania had started a mutiny in Uganda's armed forces. He fled to his driver's quarters near the State House in Kampala and tried to contact his officers, without success. If there was a revolt in progress, Amin knew his life was at stake.

The reason Amin could not find out the true story was that his officers had also fled the scene. At midnight his officers had been relaxing at a nearby hotel. The sound of gunfire from the airport sent them running for cover. They told family members not to reveal their whereabouts. Until they knew who was behind the raid, they did not want to take sides.

Later Amin learned the truth. An elite squad of Israeli commandos in four transport planes had landed at Entebbe airport at one minute past midnight. They had stormed the terminal with a lightning assault. The

Israelis celebrated when 103 hostages, who had been held for days at Uganda's Entebbe International Airport, were successfully rescued and brought back to Israel.

terrorists and Ugandan troops were taken completely by surprise. In a furious gun battle, all seven terrorists, twenty Ugandan soldiers, and three hostages were killed. The leader of the Israeli force also lost his life. Less than an hour after landing, the Israelis had gathered the remaining 103 hostages and jetted off for Tel Aviv.

Amin Takes His Revenge

The raid on Entebbe Airport quickly became news around the world. The precision of the Israelis' assault had exposed Amin's military forces as disorganized and ineffective. The Israelis had also destroyed eleven Russian-built MiG fighter planes, which was one-fourth of Amin's air force. Many Ugandans were glad to see the general and his soldiers so completely humiliated. Israel had taught the dictator a lesson.

Of course, Amin was enraged. His first instinct was to lash out at someone or something. He remembered that one hostage was still under his control: Dora Bloch. Amin ordered four members of the State Research Bureau, including its head, Major Farouk Minawa, to go to Mulago Hospital. The men shouted at the medical people to stand back as they strode the corridors. They burst into Bloch's room, grabbed her by both arms, and half-dragged her down three flights of stairs. Horrified onlookers watched as the screaming woman was forced into a car and driven away.

Later that night, Amin phoned Henry Kyemba to discuss those who were killed or wounded in the raid. At one point, he said, "Oh, by the way, that woman in hospital—don't worry about her—she has been killed."[20] When the British High Commission demanded news about Dora Bloch, Amin told his people to lie. They swore that she was taken back to the airport before the raid, that she left with the commandos. Amin forced

Kyemba to change the hospital records to hide the facts about her stay.

Shortly afterward, Bloch's dead body was dumped beside a road twenty miles from Kampala. Hundreds of Ugandans heard the news and came to view the remains. A photographer who took pictures of the scene was later

Amin's soldiers killed hostage Dora Bloch while she was hospitalized in Kampala. After her body was discovered along a road outside Kampala, Israelis brought it to Jerusalem to be buried (pictured).

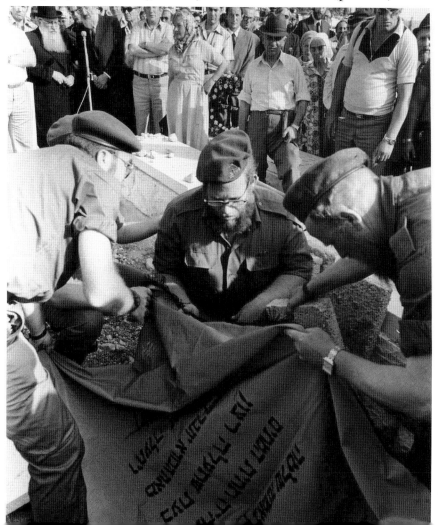

seized and shot. World opinion forced Amin to organize an investigation of Bloch's death, but as usual the facts never came out. Kyemba was never questioned. His book *A State of Blood*, published the following year, includes the first true account of Dora Bloch's murder.

Attack on Uganda's Christians

Amin's anger was slow to cool after the raid at Entebbe. The thought of people speaking of him with contempt was intolerable to him. He also realized that his soldiers were becoming dissatisfied and might revolt. Plots, coups, and assassination attempts filled his head. Fearing that his authority would slip away, he looked around for new victims to use as examples. He soon settled on the leaders of the Christian churches.

Christians, both protestant and Catholic, were a powerful majority in Uganda. As the brutality and suffering mounted, attendance at churches rose dramatically. Some pastors found subtle ways to speak out against the killings. The usual church prayers said for the leader of the country were ended in Amin's case. People looked to church leaders not only for comfort but for a way out of their nightmare.

Amin's response was to harass the Christians. He accused pastors who took donations of doing *magendo*, or business, in church. He threw Catholic missionaries out of the country. He appeared at Christian functions wearing the robes of an Arab sheik to emphasize his Muslim faith. On Christmas day, his spokesman broadcast a radio message that church leaders were preaching bloodshed, not love, from the pulpit. This final insult was too much for the Anglican archbishop, Janani Luwum, to ignore. He tried to telephone the general to register his protest, but his calls were never answered. Luwum, who was an Acholi, drew Amin's disapproval not only for his religious beliefs but also for his supposed support for his related tribesman Milton Obote.

The Bishops' Letter

Late at night in February 1977, Amin sent a group of soldiers to Luwum's house near the cathedral. The soldiers burst inside and shouted, "Show us the arms!"[21] They tore up the house searching for weapons, but none were found. It was almost dawn when the thugs left. A few days later the same treatment was given to Bishop Yona Okoth in his house. Again, nothing was found. Okoth was briefly arrested, then released.

Luwum and his bishops drew up a letter to Amin in which they described the searches and laid out, point by point, his crimes against Uganda. In the letter, the bishops wrote: "We have buried many who have died as a result of being shot and there are many more whose bodies have not been found, yet their disappearance is connected with the activities of some members of the Security Forces. Your Excellency, if it is required, we can give concrete evidence of what is happening because widows and orphans are members of our Church."[22] The letter was sent to cabinet ministers and other government officials, and several copies were smuggled out of the country. Every point in it was true, but those who read it were shocked that it was stated so boldly.

Murder of the Archbishop

A week later, Amin set up an extraordinary meeting at the Nile Hotel in Kampala. In attendance were ministers, diplomats, and church leaders, including Luwum in full robes. Television cameras were set up to capture the event. More ominously, two thousand soldiers were seated on the grounds of the hotel. In front of them were all kinds of rifles, grenades, and machine guns

Because Anglican archbishop Janani Luwum (pictured) wrote a letter that spoke out against Amin, the Ugandan leader ordered his murder.

Amin and His Wives

Through these chaotic years ran a tangled story involving Idi Amin and his changing group of wives. In March 1974, Amin suddenly divorced three of his four wives Muslim-style, by declaring publicly "I divorce thee, I divorce thee, I divorce thee." He accused the women of being antirevolutionary and of being involved in business. This was partly true, because Amin himself had given two of them textile shops to run after the Asian expulsion. The real reason for the divorces, however, was that Malyamu, Kay, and Nora had revolted against their despised husband. They complained that he spent all his time with his many mistresses, and so they took lovers of their own. This enraged the general.

Soon after the divorces, Malyamu was arrested for allegedly smuggling some cloth into Kenya. A year later, her car was rammed by Amin's agents, which left her in Mulago Hospital with serious fractures of her arm and leg. Once out of the hospital, Malyamu left for London, never to return. Her children were raised by Amin's other wives.

Amin's second wife, Kay, was not so fortunate. In August 1974, she was arrested then released for possession of a gun that Amin had given her. A week later, Kay disappeared.

Shortly afterward, her dismembered body was brought to the Mulago Hospital mortuary. Accounts differ as to how she died, and even whether Amin was responsible. Clearly, however, Amin felt no remorse about her death. Henry Kyemba reports that Amin had the body parts sewn back together for a viewing by Kay's family. During the viewing, which was televised, he shouted at his children that their mother was a bad woman.

Amin married yet again in 1975, this time to another dancer named Sarah. Sarah's boyfriend objected to the relationship, and Amin had his bodyguards dispose of him. When Sarah was unable to add to the general's twenty children, he lost interest in her.

Amin married Sarah (pictured) in 1975, one year after he divorced three of his other wives.

in neat rows. Unbeknownst to the crowd, Amin was watching everything from an upstairs balcony. The meeting had been carefully planned.

A colonel opened the meeting by announcing the discovery of a plot to overthrow General Amin's government. As evidence, several statements were read. The first was supposed to be a secret letter written by Milton Obote. Much of it was Obote's work, but parts were changed by one of Amin's associates to incriminate Amin's enemies. In the letter, the writer urged the Ugandan people to revolt. He said that a revolt should be helped along by people who were above suspicion, like Luwum and Okoth. Next, an intelligence officer and another citizen read statements in which they confessed to having received orders from Obote and shipments of the weapons that were lying on the grass. The confessions, of course, were Amin's work. The weapons did not come from Obote. They were standard issue for Uganda's army.

Amin then appeared on the balcony to ask the soldiers to raise their hands if the plotters should die. Every soldier raised his hand and shouted in Swahili, "Kill them! Kill them!" Directly after the meeting, the church leaders were ushered into the hotel. Luwum was told that Amin wanted a private meeting with him.

Instead, agents of the State Research Bureau forced the archbishop and two cabinet ministers into waiting cars. One of the ministers was a Langi tribesman, the other an Acholi—convenient scapegoats because of their ties to Obote's people. The three men were rushed to the headquarters at Nakasero Hill.

That night, a prisoner in a cell at Nakasero saw Amin arrive and go into an office. A few minutes afterward, he saw the archbishop and the two ministers being led into the same office. The official story was that Luwum and the others died in a car wreck. Henry Kyemba, however, was called to the hospital mortuary to view the bodies hours later. They were riddled with bullet holes. Amin made sure that the archbishop's funeral was held miles away from Kampala, in the small town where the archbishop had been born. Armed soldiers were ordered to guard his grave.

CHAPTER 6

THE WAR FOR UGANDA

The murder of Luwum was a major turning point for Idi Amin's regime. World opinion condemned Amin, and most countries broke diplomatic ties. Trade with Uganda was cut off by several nations, including the United States. Numerous Ugandan ministers and officials fled the country. Henry Kyemba escaped to London with his wife and family.

As usual, Amin tried to put the best face on things. At a celebration to mark the seventh anniversary of his coup, he predicted that 1978 would be a year of peace and reconciliation for Uganda. He promised

Luwum's murder caused many countries to break diplomatic ties with Uganda. At the celebration of the seventh anniversary of his coup, however, Amin promised peace and reconciliation.

reforms inside the country and better relations with Uganda's neighbors. He started a probe into the State Research Bureau, as if he wanted to clean out the murderous elements. Killings of Ugandan citizens, however, continued. A judge who had spoken out against Amin's brutality was shot by State Research Bureau agents in front of his home. Despite the promises, nothing changed.

Conflict in Amin's Inner Circle

By the spring of 1978, tensions developed in Amin's inner circle of Kakwa tribesmen. The most serious quarrel was between Amin and his brother-in-law, General Mustafa Adrisi, who was vice president as well as minister of defense. It began when one of Adrisi's relatives was shot and killed in a shady business deal. Adrisi asked Amin to find the killer, but he refused. Adrisi's resentment quickly was passed on to his elite regiments at Malire. Like Amin, he had given his soldiers special favors to win their loyalty. Adrisi also wanted to eliminate the foreign element, particularly the Sudanese, from the Ugandan army. As these were Amin's strongest allies, the general would not hear of it.

Adrisi also heard grumblings among the small Muslim community in Uganda. The elders feared that if Amin lost power, there would be a terrible backlash against

Vice president and minister of defense Mustafa Adrisi (left) tried unsuccessfully to convince Amin to change his military government to a civilian one.

Muslims. They begged Adrisi to reason with Amin and convince him to change his military government to some kind of civilian rule. Adrisi did make the suggestion, which angered Amin even more.

Soon thereafter, Adrisi was badly injured in a car accident—widely believed to be an attempted murder. The vice president was flown to Cairo, Egypt, for medical treatment. Amin seized the opportunity to strip Adrisi of his power, but then, fearing a mutiny among Adrisi's followers, he reinstated the vice president.

At the same time, Amin faced other problems. The worldwide price of coffee plummeted, which shrank the profits from Uganda's top export. Libya and other Muslim countries began to ask questions about the large donations they had made to Uganda. The payments were supposed to be used to build mosques and promote Islam, but the money had disappeared. At a meeting, Amin blamed his finance minister, Moses Ali, for the losses. Amin threw an ashtray at Ali's head, and the minister drew a pistol on Amin. Other officials separated the two before there was bloodshed.

Amin's Troops Enter Tanzania

True to his usual pattern, Amin sought a way to divert attention from these conflicts. He settled on a war as the answer. In October 1978, Radio Uganda broadcast reports that Tanzanian troops, with the help of Cuban soldiers, had invaded Uganda. The reports were lies, but they served Amin as an excuse for action. At the end of October, three thousand Ugandan troops spilled over the border into the Tanzanian province of Kagera. This was a lush, thickly populated area on the western side of Lake Victoria. Uganda's army met almost no resistance. For some reason, Tanzania's president Nyerere had neglected to defend the border that separated his country from chaotic Uganda and its bloodthirsty ruler. The mistake had terrible consequences. One day later, Amin announced that the 710 square miles of Kagera had been added to Uganda. He warned Tanzanian troops not to cross the Kagera River or his air force would strike targets throughout their country.

Once inside Tanzania, Ugandan troops went on a rampage. They killed hundreds of unarmed civilians and smashed homes, factories, sawmills, and warehouses. Soldiers looted with abandon. Huge herds of cattle were stolen and led back to Uganda. Amin visited the site of this slaughter to pose for photographs with his troops.

In October 1978, Amin sent troops to Tanzania to divert attention from the internal problems that plagued Uganda.

Tanzania's president Julius Nyerere refused to negotiate with Amin when Ugandan troops invaded Tanzania.

Characteristically, he treated the situation as a joke. He said, "I challenge President Nyerere in the boxing ring to fight it out there rather than that soldiers lose their lives on the field of battle."[23] He added that the perfect referee for the match would be American heavyweight champion Muhammad Ali.

Tanzania's military was slow to respond. Its units were scattered around the country, and it took time for them to travel hundreds of miles. In addition, the rainy season had just begun, and the roads quickly became rivers of mud. Nyerere had other worries as well. His small army had never been in an actual conflict. No one knew how his troops would respond. Nyerere doubted whether they could repel Amin's professional soldiers.

Tanzania Fights Back

The situation in Kagera rapidly became a crisis for all of Africa. Nations of the Organization of African Unity urged Amin to withdraw his army at once. Amin said he would do so only if he got guarantees that Tanzania would not invade his country again. Amin also had some success playing regional politics. He told his fellow African leaders that the weapons Tanzania was using against his army were bought by OAU states for use against South Africa's racist government. Believing these lies, some leaders criticized Tanzania and made excuses for Amin.

When Amin refused to leave Kagera, the OAU suggested that a compromise might be worked out. Nyerere was outraged. "Do you negotiate with a burglar

Amin, pictured here as he fires a rocket launcher, encouraged his troops to loot and brutally murder Tanzanians.

when he is in your house?"[24] he asked. Nyerere, one of the founders of the OAU, was amazed at how reluctant the OAU nations were to condemn Amin's actions. With no concrete support from the international community, he became determined to kick out the invaders himself.

When Tanzanian forces reached Kagera, they surrounded the Ugandans and slowly pushed them back across the border. Amin's troops continued to murder and loot as they retreated. In fact, their behavior became even more brutal than during the invasion. More than two thousand women and children were taken prisoner, and hundreds were killed. It was this brazen disregard for the Tanzanian population that set the course for the rest of the war. Tanzanians were full of rage. They wanted Nyerere to pursue this conflict to the end.

Nyerere's Decision

After Amin's troops crossed the border back into Uganda, the world's nations urged Tanzania to stop fighting. The OAU wanted a cease-fire, but it still would not condemn Idi Amin's invasion. Nyerere fumed, "Do we then say 'fine' and he gets away with it? This is not simply a situation where the aggressor gets away with it. It is a situation where Tanzanians would have paid for that aggression."[25] Nyerere ordered his troops to continue to the barracks in southern Uganda where the brutal battalions came from. Once those troops who had pillaged his country were dealt with and his borders were safe, he planned to withdraw. He made it clear that he would love to see Amin overthrown, but that was not his country's goal.

As Tanzania's forces advanced into Uganda, they were met by grateful citizens who urged them on. Ugandan troops had continued to smash and murder on their way back, this time terrorizing their own people. Amin broadcast threats against anyone who welcomed the enemy, but his words sounded hollow. Ugandans in the south could feel his grip on power slipping away. Amin grew desperate at this turn of events. He begged his friend Gadhafi to

When Tanzanian troops entered Uganda, thousands of grateful Ugandans walked alongside them and greeted them with cheers and celebrations.

send help. In response, the Libyan leader gave Tanzania twenty-four hours to leave Uganda or else Libyan troops would enter the battle. For Nyerere, this was the last straw. He refused to bow to Libya's threats. He also did not want to abandon Uganda's people to another wave of Amin's murderous revenge. Tanzanian forces would not stop until they reached Kampala.

The Fall of Kampala

Gadhafi did indeed send troops to aid Amin, but they were ineffective. Trained in desert fighting, they were bewildered by the swamps, bush, and forests of Uganda. Tanzania's soldiers, by contrast, were trained to march long distances in any terrain. Time and again they were able to surround the Libyans and defeat them. By now, the Tanzanian forces had been joined by more than a thousand Ugandan exiles. Along the way, they added rifles and ammunition that the Ugandan troops dropped on the ground as they ran. Jubilant people in the countryside greeted them with each advance.

Amin's tactics in the war were mystifying. His troops kept retreating and smashing everything in their path. Tanzanian forces proceeded with caution, but never had to make a concentrated attack. It was as though Uganda's army had no chain of command and no plan of defense. Amin flew between troop positions by helicopter and threatened to have deserters shot. He raged over the radio and promised a rapid victory. To try to win support from Arab nations, he insisted that the Tanzanians were targeting Muslims in their advance. His

On their way to Kampala, Tanzanian forces, joined by Ugandan exiles, picked up rifles and ammunition dropped by retreating Ugandans.

desperate words had no effect. He was helpless to prevent the unraveling of his poorly led army.

In March 1979, the end was in sight. Ugandan exile groups met at Moshi in northeastern Tanzania to discuss what kind of government would follow Amin's fall. The groups formed the Uganda National Liberation Front (UNLF) in hopes of orchestrating a smooth transfer of power. Milton Obote, who had consulted with Nyerere throughout the war, was left out of the UNLF's plans. It was feared that the former Ugandan leader would stir up the same opposition as when he ruled eight years before.

Kampala, the capital city, was taken after only a few bursts of artillery. Thousands of Ugandans met the

Tanzanian troops with cheers. They sang songs and beat drums, much as they had when Amin took power. Colonel Ben Msuya, the Tanzanian commander, learned that Amin and his guards had fled the city the day before.

The End of Amin's Rule

When Kampala fell, two of the Ugandan exiles fighting alongside the Tanzanians broadcast messages to the people over Radio Uganda. They announced that Amin's rule was over and a new provisional government was being formed. Amin replied with his own broadcast from somewhere in eastern Uganda. He seemed confused, his English more broken than usual. At first he said the rebels were on a killing spree all over the country, but then he said they were a small force that was really no threat. "They have killed very many innocent Ugandans, children, young and old, and women," he said. "Destroying the whole Kampala including the Mulago Hospital, killing doctors, nurses. Making the mercenaries tyrannizing the people of Uganda. Even changing completely the town of Uganda today. It is not as a town, therefore I am surprised this so-called government wanted to form a government in Uganda after killing everyone."[26] Amin assured his listeners that he was still in control of the country.

Tanzanian troops slowly searched through Amin's headquarters and prisons in Kampala. At the State Research Bureau, they found piles of corpses and a few skeletal prisoners still alive in the dungeons under Nakasero Hill. At a Kampala warehouse, they discovered mountains of sugar in bags. Amin had used it to barter for arms with Libya. The citizens of Kampala had gone without sugar for more than a year. When the people began to loot Amin's buildings, the Tanzanians simply left them to their work.

When Tanzanian troops searched the State Research Bureau, they found secret files, a few prisoners who were still alive, and piles of corpses in the dungeons.

The end came in Idi Amin's home territory, in Arua and the West Nile district. Tanzanian troops followed Amin's escaping Nubian and Sudanese soldiers, who continued to loot and murder along the way. Msuya expected a climactic battle in the northwest, but aside from a few skirmishes, his soldiers were unopposed. In the towns they were again greeted with flowers, singing, and drumming as welcome liberators. Amin's soldiers had already melted away across the border into Zaire and Sudan. The war was over, and Idi Amin's rule of Uganda was officially at an end.

Amin in Exile

At the invitation of Libya's Muammar Gadhafi, Idi Amin escaped to Libya in June 1979, reportedly with two wives and twenty-four children. Amin hoped to trade on his loyalty as a Muslim. By the end of the year, however, he had angered his host. His personal security guards quarreled and fought with Libyan police, and Amin was asked to leave. He then accepted an offer of asylum in Saudi Arabia.

In 1989, Amin attempted to return to Uganda. He was recognized by sentries in Kinshasa, Zaire, and forced to go back to his home in Saudi Arabia. He resumed his comfortable life with family members in the town of

After the overthrow of his government, Idi Amin escaped to Libya. He was eventually offered asylum in Saudi Arabia, where he lived until his death in 2003.

Jeddah on the Red Sea. Diplomats in Saudi Arabia often spotted him sipping coffee with fellow Ugandan exiles on a shady terrace at the Hotel Al Waha. Amin also liked to watch soccer and rugby games on satellite television, play the organ, and swim and fish at a resort near the Yemeni border.

In the summer of 2003, Amin was hospitalized with numerous health problems. He soon slipped into a coma and died on August 16, 2003. Amin was buried in a Muslim cemetery after sunset prayers. His relatives claimed that the Ugandan government had refused to allow his burial in Uganda. A government spokesperson denied the stories.

Epilogue

Amin's brutal eight-year rule in Uganda left more than three hundred thousand dead. His legacy of torture cells and firing squads will never be erased from the national memory. Nearly every citizen shared in the horror from the death of friends or loved ones. Fear and distrust were sown deeply into the minds of the people. Terrible as it was, however, the death toll is only part of the story. As a result of Amin's folly as a leader, Uganda fell from one of Africa's great economic successes to a land ravaged with shortages, inflation, and wrecked industries. Amin's policies reportedly left Uganda with a debt of more than $250 million. The economic pain extended to the entire region, as trade was disrupted and refugees from Uganda ate

For more than twenty years, Uganda has struggled to recover from Amin's reign, which brought death, horror, and poverty to the "pearl of Africa."

up resources in neighboring countries. Disease also spread wildly, first from the refugees, then from Amin's vicious troops.

Since Amin's overthrow, Uganda has struggled to recover. Milton Obote returned to power in the early 1980s, but his government was a failure. Inept governments and sporadic civil wars plagued the country in the 1980s. AIDS also became a major problem, with an estimated 1.5 million Ugandans infected with the virus. Yet in recent years, the country has seen signs of stability, and some of its talented exiles have returned.

Idi Amin, one of the world's most brutal dictators, was never tried for his crimes.

CHRONOLOGY

ca. 1925	Idi Amin is born in West Nile district of Uganda.
1946	Amin joins King's African Rifles.
1951	Amin becomes Uganda's heavyweight boxing champion.
March 1962	Self-government in Uganda.
October 9, 1962	Uganda gains independence.
1966	Amin leads troops in battle against King Freddie.
December 19, 1969	Attempt on Obote's life; Amin flees.
January 25, 1970	Brigadier Okoya and his wife are shot; Amin is suspected.
January 25, 1971	Amin leads successful coup.
March 1971	Obote supporters in the military are massacred.
February 1972	Amin visits Gadhafi in Tripoli, Libya.
March 1972	Amin severs ties with Israel.
August 5, 1972	Amin orders Asians to leave Uganda.
November 1972	Amin begins distributing Asians' property.
1973	Libya begins training Uganda's military.
March 1974	Michael Ondoga is murdered.

August 1974	Kay Amin's dismembered body is found.
1975	Amin is elected president of OAU.
July 4, 1976	Israel raids Entebbe to free hostages.
July 5, 1976	Dora Bloch is murdered.
February 17, 1977	Archbishop Luwum is arrested and murdered.
March 1977	Many countries cut off relations with Uganda.
October 1978	Amin sends Ugandan troops into Tanzania.
April 1979	Tanzanian troops take Kampala.
June 1979	Tanzania wins the war; Amin flees Uganda.
1980	Amin settles in Saudi Arabia.
1989	Amin unsuccessfully tries to return to Uganda.

GLOSSARY

allegiance Loyalty.

apartheid Strict racial segregation.

armory Place where weapons are kept.

coalition Temporary alliance for an agreed-upon action.

commodity A product of agriculture.

coup A sudden, violent overthrow of a government.

dictator Leader who wields absolute power.

guerrilla Fighter who engages in irregular warfare including sabotage.

martial law Law administered by military forces.

protectorate Nation under the control of another, usually more powerful one.

regime A government in power.

SOURCE NOTES

Chapter 1: Independence for Uganda

1. George Ivan Smith, *Ghosts of Kampala*. New York: St. Martin's, 1980, p. 46.

2. Quoted in Siraje Lubwama, "Idi Amin's Untold Story," *Kampala Monitor*, April 11, 1999.

3. Henry Kyemba, *A State of Blood*. New York: Ace, 1977, p. 24.

Chapter 2: Amin Takes Control

4. Quoted in David Martin, "Horror in Uganda," *New York Review of Books*, September 16, 1976.

5. Quoted in Afrol News, April 7, 2001. www.afrol.com.

6. Quoted in Afrol News.

Chapter 3: The Expulsion of the Asians

7. Quoted in Martin, "Horror in Uganda."

8. Quoted in Smith, *Ghosts of Kampala*, p. 103.

9. Quoted in Trevor Grundy, "If Only the Queen Had Asked Him to Tea," *Daily Telegraph*, August 2, 2002.

10. Quoted in Grundy, "If Only the Queen Had Asked Him to Tea."

11. Quoted in Grundy, "If Only the Queen Had Asked Him to Tea."

Chapter 4: Clown and Tyrant

12. Quoted in Smith, *Ghosts of Kampala*, p. 105.

13. Quoted in Smith, *Ghosts of Kampala*, pp. 105–106.

14. Quoted in Smith, *Ghosts of Kampala*, p. 105.

15. Quoted in Barbet Schroeder, *Idi Amin Dada*. Criterion Video, 1980.

16. Godfrey Lule, in foreword to Kyemba, *A State of Blood*, p. 7.

17. Kyemba, *A State of Blood*.

18. Quoted in Smith, *Ghosts of Kampala*, p. 106.

Chapter 5: The Entebbe Raid

19. Kyemba, *A State of Blood*, p. 169.

20. Quoted in Kyemba, *A State of Blood*, p. 175.

21. Quoted in Kyemba, *A State of Blood*, p. 180.

22. Quoted in Kyemba, *A State of Blood*, p. 274.

Chapter 6: The War for Uganda

23. Quoted in Smith, *Ghosts of Kampala*, p. 180.

24. Quoted in Smith, *Ghosts of Kampala*, p. 106.

25. Quoted in Tony Avirgan and Martha Honey, *War in Uganda: The Legacy of Idi Amin*. Westport, CT: Lawrence Hill, 1982, p. 77.

26. Quoted in Avirgan and Honey, *War in Uganda*, p. 147.

FOR MORE INFORMATION

Books

Tony Avirgan and Martha Honey, *War in Uganda: The Legacy of Idi Amin*. Westport, CT: Lawrence Hill, 1982.

Robert Barlas, *Uganda*. Benchmark, 2000.

Ettagale Blauer and Jason Laure, *Uganda*. Childrens, 1997.

Kenneth Ingham, *Obote: A Political Biography*. London and New York: Routledge, 1994.

Henry Kyemba, *A State of Blood*. New York: Ace, 1977.

George Ivan Smith, *Ghosts of Kampala*. New York: St. Martin's, 1980.

Websites

Idi Amin Dada Oumee (www.moreorless.au.com/killers/amin.htm). An overview of Amin's life.

Uganda History (http://enteruganda.com). Good site for historical background of Uganda.

INDEX

PICTURE CREDITS